Songs

OF THE

Suffragists

LYRICS OF AMERICAN FEMINISM
FROM 1850 TO 2020

The League of Women Voters
Berkeley Heights, New Providence & Summit
Written by Laura Engelhardt and Stephanie Lioudis

Copyright © 2020 The League of Women Voters Berkeley Heights,
New Providence & Summit. All rights reserved.

Cover design by: Anna Burrous
Print Layout by: Booknook.Biz

ISBN 9781711686431

Songs of the Suffragists: Lyrics of American Feminism from 1850 to 2020
was written by Laura Engelhardt and Stephanie Lioudis

Cover Photo: Carrie Chapman Catt (center), founder of the League of Women Voters, and Dr. Anna Shaw (left) leading approximately 20,000 supporters in a New York City women's suffrage march in 1917. AP

suf·frage: the right to vote in political elections

This book is dedicated to all the unsung heroes who worked with diligence and courage to win the right to vote for women

Acknowledgments

Songs of the Suffragists: Lyrics of American Feminism from 1850 to 2020 was conceived of, researched, and drafted by the LWV-BHNPS's stellar group of 2018 and 2019 interns: Bridget Bowen, Julia Haas, Stephanie Lioudis, and Elizabeth Moshkevich. Each brought their unique insight and perspective to the creation of this book. But for their vision and talent, this book would not have come to be. We owe special thanks to the Intellectual Property Law Clinic of Rutgers University, and in particular to Sabrina Bazelais, Vincent Delriccio and Jason Tarella, who provided us with copyright guidance and advice. Finally, we are grateful for the creative direction provided by League members, Pat Dolan, Laura Engelhardt and Susan Ferris Rights.

Contents

The Significance of Suffrage Music 2

"The Bloomer's Complaint" 4

"Battle Hymn of the Republic" and "Dare You Do It" 6

"Human Equality" and "Daughters of Freedom! The Ballot Be Yours" 8

"Shall Women Vote?" 10

"Oh, Dear, What Can the Matter Be?" 12

"Eliza Jane" 14

"Three Blind Men" 16

"The March of the Women" 18

"How Can Such Things Be?" 20

"The Anti-Suffrage Rose" 22

"She's Good Enough to Be Your Baby's Mother" 24

"Rosie the Riveter" 30

"You Don't Own Me" 32

"Four Women" 34

"Respect" and "I Am Woman" 36

"The Pill" 38

"Standing on the Shoulders" and "Rebel Girl" 40

"Hijabi" 42

"Woman" 44

    Postlude 46

    References 48

    About the League of Women Voters 57

Songs

of the

Suffragists

The Significance of Suffrage Music

SINCE THE VERY FOUNDING OF the United States, activists have spoken out for women's rights. In 1776, Abigail Adams famously wrote to her husband, asking him to "remember the ladies," when considering the laws that would govern our new country. But despite such Early appeals, it wasn't until 1920 that the federal government extended the franchise to women. One hundred years later, activists are still seeking to transform the United States into an equal society for women and men.

At the time the U.S. Constitution was drafted, universal suffrage was far from the norm. In fact, many colonies limited the franchise to white, Protestant men who owned property or paid taxes, and the Constitution left to the states the decision of which of its citizens could vote. While many states gradually removed religious and property-based limitations on white male suffrage, it wasn't until the mid-1800s that the movement to enfranchise women really began.

Movements for social and political change have long depended on cultural messages to persuade and unite people behind new ideas. The women's suffrage movement leveraged songs, posters, plays, books, and even apparel to convince people that granting women the right to vote was necessary. Songs were written to unify supporters of women's suffrage, persuade the public and to ridicule opponents. While some songs were intended to be read as opposed to performed, others were set to popular music and sung at rallies and during marches. The medium of song has been a critical aspect of the women's equality movement, from the days of the original suffragists through the modern era.

This book provides a snapshot of the women's movement in the United States through song: from first-wave feminism (the suffrage movement), where songs focused on the morality of the suffragist cause, likening the lack of franchise to a lack of freedom, through the second-wave feminism of the post-WWII era (where activists and songs focused on social equality, including reproductive rights), to the so-called third-wave feminism of the late twentieth century (characterized by efforts to dismantle systemic barriers to gender equality) and the modern feminism of the new millennium (where activists are focusing on female empowerment and ending sexual violence).

While modern feminist songs are recorded and performed, reaching a broad audience, the songs of the original suffragists were published in newspapers and on broadsheets. Many were produced for local audiences, and some of the songs were manifesto-like essays in verse. Reactionary songs were written by anti-suffragists to mock activists and warn of dire consequences that would result from any effort to change the social order.

Whether intended to be performed or read, feminist songs sought to advance the cause of equality through cultural and political change. Changes in law cannot endure without corresponding changes in popular beliefs. The songs of the suffragists were written to shape popular opinion and attitudes, as well as to fight for women's equality through changes in law.

Throughout the years, the themes and tools of feminist protest movements have remained constant: from the prohibitionists who proclaimed "lips that touch liquor shall never touch mine," to Alyssa Milano's call for a "sex strike" in opposition to punitive anti-abortion laws. From the proponents of the rational dress movement who proclaimed they would do as they please, to the 1960s woman who sang that she was also free to say and do whatever she pleased. From the abolitionists who used the language of Christian morality in support of freedom, to the suffragists and pro-choice activists who used similar moral arguments in support of their causes. These proponents of change leveraged the same language to win hearts and minds, and this book highlights the many similarities in feminist songs from 1850 to 2020.

American women have consistently advocated for changes in law and in culture to make our society a more equal place for all. We hope you enjoy this history of the U.S. feminist movement through the songs of the suffragists.

Six suffragists (including Alice Paul, second from right) gathered
with a banner at the 1920 Republican National Convention.
(Library of Congress, Manuscript Division)

"The Bloomer's Complaint"

By the mid-1800s, the movement for women's equality in the United States and the United Kingdom was well under way. Many women who became suffragists began their activist careers in the abolitionist movement. Although American women were often impassioned anti-slavery advocates, their role in the movement was limited on the basis of their gender. After Lucretia Mott and Elizabeth Cady Stanton were barred from attending the World Anti-Slavery Convention in London in 1840, they sponsored their own Women's Convention, which met in Seneca Falls, New York. At this convention, Elizabeth Cady Stanton presented "The Declaration of Sentiments," modeled after the Declaration of Independence, but focusing on women's independence. States began extending property rights to women in 1839, and by 1900, all states had passed laws to recognize the property rights of married women.

As women began making strides towards political independence, the feminist movement also expressed itself through women's fashion. "Bloomers" were a new style of pants pioneered in the mid-1800s by suffragists Amelia Bloomer and Elizabeth Smith Miller. These pants were more loose fitting than other clothing of the day, allowing women the freedom of movement to pursue activities like bicycle riding. As seen with other shifts in women's fashion tied to changing social mores in recent times (*e.g.* mini-skirts in the 1960s and activewear in the 2010s), there was a significant backlash to bloomers in the latter half of the nineteenth century. Bloomer-wearing women were ridiculed and berated for their attire. "The Bloomer's Complaint" reflects this public backlash against women's independence. But similar to Lesley Gore's 1963 proclamation that "You Don't Own Me," the Bloomer of this 1851 song intends to "do, after all, as she pleases."

David M. Rubenstein Rare Book and Manuscript Library at Duke University, 1851.

"The Bloomer's Complaint"
Published by A. Fiot
1851

Dear me, what a terrible clatter they raise,
Because that old gossip Dame Rumor
Declares, with her hands lifted up in amaze,
That I'm coming out as a Bloomer,
That I'm coming out as a Bloomer.
I wonder how often these men must be told
When a woman a notion once seizes,
However they ridicule, lecture or scold,
She'll do, after all, as she pleases,
She'll do, after all, as she pleases.

They know very well that their own fashions change
With each little change of the season,
But Oh! it is "monstrous" and "dreadful" and "strange"
And "out of all manner of reason,"
And "out of all manner of reason"
If we take a fancy to alter our dress,
And come out in style "a la Bloomer,"
To hear what an outcry they make, I confess
Is putting me quite out of humor,
Is putting me quite out of humor.

I'll come out next week, with a wide Bloomer flat
Of a shape that I fancy will fright them,
I had not intended to go quite to that,
But I'll do it now, only to spite them,
But I'll do it now, only to spite them
With my pants "a la Turque" and my skirts two feet long
All fitting of course, most completely
These grumblers shall own after all, they are wrong,
And that I, in a Bloomer, look sweetly,
And that I, in a Bloomer, look sweetly.

"Battle Hymn of the Republic" and "Dare You Do It"

JULIA WARD HOWE WAS A suffragist songwriter who began publishing poems, essays and plays in the mid-1800s. She is most famous for her song, the "Battle Hymn of the Republic," written in 1861 and set to the tune of "John Brown's Body." Many suffragists began their activist careers in the other significant social change movements of their times: abolitionism and temperance. For instance, while Harriet Tubman is best known for her heroism as a conductor in the underground railroad, she also spoke out in favor of women's suffrage, and was considered a spellbinding orator on the suffrage circuit.

Portrait of Julia Ward Howe, 1887, inducted into the Songwriters Hall of Fame in 1970. (Image source unknown)

The "Battle Hymn of the Republic" was a popular and highly influential abolitionist song that inspired many other activist songs. The theme of the "Battle Hymn of the Republic" is the moral urgency and godly nature of the Union cause based on the abolition of slavery. In 1890, a women's rights activist penned the "Battle Hymn of the Suffragists," which cried: "They come from every nation, women fair and strong and brave." By using the same highly popular tune from the abolitionist movement, pro-suffrage songwriters leveraged the same spirit and moral urgency that inspired many to join the abolitionist cause in their efforts to stir support for women's suffrage.

The Civil War ended in the spring of 1865, and on May 10, 1866, Elizabeth Cady Stanton and Susan B. Anthony formed the American Equal Rights Association, with the goal of achieving universal suffrage, irrespective of race or gender. After the Civil War, other groups also formed to advance gender equality, including Julia Ward Howe's American Woman Suffrage Association. During the 1868 presidential election, 172 women cast ballots in a separate box in Vineland, New Jersey. The women brought their own ballot box (made out of blueberry crates) after Portia Gage had been prevented from voting the previous spring.

Songs of the Suffragists

Excerpt from **"Battle Hymn of the Republic"**
Lyrics by Julia Ward Howe
1862

Mine eyes have seen the glory of the coming of the Lord;
He is trampling out the vintage where the grapes of wrath are stored;
He hath loosed the fateful lightning of His terrible swift sword;
His truth is marching on.
Chorus:
Glory! Glory! Hallelujah!
Glory! Glory! Hallelujah!
Glory! Glory! Hallelujah!
His truth is marching on.
…
I have read a fiery gospel writ in burnished rows of steel:
"As ye deal with my contemners, so with you my grace shall deal";
Let the Hero, born of woman, crush the serpent with his heel,
Since God is marching on
…

He has sounded forth the trumpet
That shall never call retreat;
He is sifting out the hearts of men
Before His judgement seat;
Oh, be swift, my soul, to answer Him!
Be jubilant, my feet!
Our God is marching on.
…
In the beauty of the lilies Christ was born across the sea,
With a glory in His bosom that transfigures you and me.
As He died to make men holy,
Let us die to make men free,
While God is marching on.

Excerpt from **"Dare You Do It"**
Lyrics by Henry Roby
1909

Ye men who wrong your mothers,
And your wives and sisters, too,
How dare you rob companions
Who are always brave and true?
How dare you make them servants
Who are all the world to you,
As they go marching on?

Chorus:
Men and brothers, dare you do it?
Men and brothers, dare you do it?
Men and brothers, dare you do it?
As we go marching on?

Whence came your foolish notion
Now so greatly overgrown
That a woman's sober judgment
Is not equal to your own?
Has God ordained that suffrage
Is a gift to you alone,
While life goes marching on?

Chorus.

"Humanity Equality" and "Daughters of Freedom! The Ballot Be Yours"

BY 1870, THE ESSENTIAL GOALS of the abolitionist movement had been achieved. The Thirteenth Amendment prohibiting slavery was passed in 1865, followed by the Fourteenth Amendment in 1868, which guaranteed equal protection of law to all citizens. After the Fifteenth Amendment gave black men the right to vote in 1870, the women's suffrage movement went into full swing, as many abolitionists refocused their political activism on the other large-scale activist movements of their time: the temperance and suffrage movements.

The 1871 songs, "Human Equality" by William Lloyd Garrison and "Daughters of Freedom! The Ballot Be Yours," by George Cooper advocated for women's rights, starting with the franchise. "Human Equality" was a manifesto in song-form and was originally published in Garrison's paper, *The Liberator*. It sets forth the radical view that all people are equal, with no one granted God-given power over others. "Daughters of Freedom! The Ballot Be Yours" was written as a rallying cry in favor of female suffrage. It was dedicated to Mary Livermore, an abolitionist, suffragist and prolific writer. She served as a nurse in the Civil War and published her seven hundred-page memoirs in 1899, which provide an autobiographical account of pre-Civil War life in the North and South.

In 1872, Victoria Woodhull campaigned as a candidate for President for the Equal Rights Party. Although her candidacy was not taken seriously by the public, she became the first woman to address a House committee when she argued that the Fourteenth and Fifteenth Amendments granted women the right to vote. While two representatives were persuaded, the request that Congress draft legislation granting women the vote did not pass to the House floor.

Victoria Woodhull, between 1866 and 1873. (Harvard Art Museum/Fogg Museum)

Excerpt from **"Human Equality"**
Lyrics by William Lloyd Garrison
1871

There is no king by right divine
To rule and reign and a' that:
No princely rank, nor lordly line—
Equality for a' that!
Dynastic power, and a' that,
A common birthright crowns us all
With liberty, for a' that

Let fools and upstarts boast they find
In ancestry, and a' that,
A higher place to them assigned—
Mankind are one, for a' that!
For a' that, and a' that,
A pompous air, and a' that:
It matters not how born of bred,
We're one for blood for a' that!

Though woman never can be man,
By change of sex and a' that,
To equal rights, 'gainst class or clan,
Her claim is just for a' that!
For a' that, and a' that:
In all that makes a living soul
She matches man, for a' that!
She asks no favors at his hands,
On bended knee, and a' that;

She is his peer where'er he stands,
In spite of sex, and a' that.
For a' that, and a' that,
Fair play for her, and a' that,
In all the grave concerns of life—
This is her due for a' that …

"Daughters of Freedom! The Ballet Be Yours"
Music by Edwin Christie
Lyrics by George Cooper
1871 © 1897

Daughters of freedom arise in your might!
March to the watchwords Justice and Right!
Why will ye slumber? wake, O wake!
Lo! on your legions light doth break!

Chorus:
Sunder the fetters "custom" hath made!
Come from the valley, hill and glade!

Daughters of freedom, the truth marches on,
Yield not the battle till ye have won!
Heed not the "corner," day by day
Clouds of oppression roll away!

Chorus
Daughters of freedom, the truth marches on,
Yield not the battle till ye have won!
Heed not the "scorner," day by day
Clouds of oppression roll away!

Chorus
Daughters of freedom, the "Ballot" be yours,
Wield it with wisdom, your hopes it
    secures.
"Rights that are equal" – this ye claim,
Bright by your guerdon, fair your fame!

"Shall Women Vote?"

AFTER THE CIVIL WAR, WOMEN played leading activist roles in the temperance movement, which ultimately led to prohibition in 1919 with the adoption of the Eighteenth Amendment. Temperance proponents argued that much of the pervasive domestic violence against women and children stemmed from alcohol use and abuse. The Woman's Christian Temperance Union was formed in 1874, quickly becoming the largest women's organization in the nation. Frances Willard, then president of the WCTU, advocated for suffrage in 1879 as a means of achieving the conservative Christian agenda.

Just a few years before the WCTU was formed, Congress received its first proposed amendment for women's suffrage in 1868. While not passed in 1868, or again in 1878 or 1914 when re-introduced, the Nineteenth Amendment as ultimately passed fifty years later, used nearly identical language to the original proposal.

Songs were a critical part of suffrage rallies in the late 1880s. In 1880, "Keep Woman in her Sphere," set to the tune of "Auld Lang Syne," applauded the opinion of an "earnest, thoughtful man" who believed "'Her rights are just the same as mine, / Let woman choose her sphere.'"

"The Lips That Touch Liquor Shall Never Touch Mine," a song of the temperance movement, 1874. (Library of Congress, Music Division)

The following year, the lyricist of "Shall Women Vote?" likened the roles of women to that of slaves, echoing the moral arguments of abolition in an effort to galvanize people to the cause of women's suffrage. The fourth verse opines that we cannot speak of "freedom" and "equal rights" when twenty million slaves (*i.e.* women) remain in our country. Similar to the prohibitionists, suffragists appealed to people's Christianity in an effort to persuade them ("For the love pow'r is the strongest ... Its author, God is love"). As with the abolitionist songs of past decades, "Shall Women Vote?" proclaims the morality of the pro-suffrage cause using Christian imagery. Suffragists, in the eyes of this author, are on the side of the angels.

"Shall Women Vote?"

Lyrics by Joseph D. Payne
Music by Frank Boylen
1881

Shall women vote, we answer, yes,
How could we answer no,
And boast of freedom in our midst,
Without entailing woe.
Why should they not plug ugly, tell,
What rights have you to claim,
That they have not with right, as well,
To ask, demand the same.

Chorus:
For the love pow'r is the strongest,
In earth, or heav'n above,
With harmony surrounded,
Its author, God is love!

Does might make right, is this your plea,
If so please stand aside,
The elephant will take the front,
Our ship of state to guide.
Is it because that you can drink
More whiskey, beer, and wine,
And not get drunk, and seem to think
Your majesty divine?

Chorus

Is it because you look so wise,
And say big words of love
While beams from out those blood
    streak'd eyes
The words, my dear, my dove?
A serpent knew the pow'r of love,
Six thousand years ago,
And did he to your sex appeal?
The echo, answers no!

Chorus

Talk not of freedom, equal rights,
Cold hearted, selfish knaves,
While in our land, around our hearths,
Dwell twenty million slaves.
Love, justice, liberty, demands,
That they should be set free,
Can you such pow'rs as these withstand,
And claim consistency?

Chorus

The past and present all combine,
To prove this pow'r of love,
And show its origin divine,
Descending from above.
Then wield your pow'r angelic choir,
'till earth and heav'n combine
to place your rights beyond dispute,
and prove the pow'r divine

Library of Congress,
Music Division, 1881.

Songs of the Suffragists

"Oh, Dear, What Can the Matter Be?"

PRO-SUFFRAGE SONGS CONTINUED TO BE published throughout the late 1800s, often set to familiar tunes, and often intended to be humorous or ironic. The song, "Oh, Dear, What Can the Matter Be?" was set to the tune of the popular nursery rhyme, "Oh, Dear! What Can the Matter Be?" At first glance, this song appears to be an anti-suffrage song, declaring that women already have all that they need. They have friends and community, husbands who protect them, and sons who direct them. Women have the ability to preach to the sinners, the ability to work and travel, so "[w]hy are they wanting the vote?" The first few verses recite many of the common arguments against suffrage at the time before pointing out all the ways women's labor is equal to men's. The final twist comes in the last line: "Oh, dear, what can the matter be? When *men* want every vote. [emphasis added]"

But even as pro-suffrage songs pointed out the injustice created by women's inability to participate directly in our democracy, many feared that women's suffrage would lead to the destruction of the "natural order." In 1872, the Anti-Suffrage Party was founded to block women from achieving suffrage and political equality. Like the suffragists, the anti-suffragists also employed songs and cartoons to persuade Americans that women's suffrage was dangerous, that it would lead to women abandoning their role as mothers and keepers of the home. Cartoons illustrated the fear that female suffrage would lead to emasculation. While suffrage proponents were circulating songs like "Oh, Dear, What Can the Matter Be?," anti-suffragists were also using popular culture to try to sway popular opinion against women's rights.

Anti-Suffrage postcard portraying a husband having to take on the childrearing duties, 1907. (Palczewski, Catherine H. Postcard Archive, University of Northern Iowa)

"Oh, Dear, What Can the Matter Be?"
Lyrics by L. May Wheeler
1884

Oh, dear, what can the matter be?
Dear, dear, what can the matter be?
Oh, dear, what can the matter be?
Women are wanting the vote.

Women have husbands, they are protected,
Women have sons by whom they're directed,
Women have fathers — they're not neglected,
Why are they wanting to vote?

Women have homes, there they should labor,
Women have children, whom they should favor,
Women have time to learn of each neighbor,
Why are they wanting to vote?

Women can dress, they love society,
Women have cash, with its variety,
Women can pray, with sweetest piety,
Why are they wanting to vote?

Women are preaching to sinners today,
Women are healing the sick by the way,
Women are dealing out law as they may,
Why are they wanting to vote?

Women are trav'ling about, here and there,
Women are working like men everywhere,
Women are crowding — then claiming 'tis fair,
Why are they wanting to vote?

Women have reared all the sons of the brave,
Women have shared in the burdens they gave,
Women have labored your country to save,
That's why we're wanting to vote!

Oh, dear, what can the matter be?
Dear, dear, what can the matter be?
Oh, dear, what can the matter be?
When men want every vote.

"Eliza Jane"

"ELIZA JANE," PUBLISHED IN 1895, echoes the public backlash against "masculine" attire referenced in "The Bloomer's Complaint." "The personal is political" wasn't simply a slogan of the 1960s, but instead underscores an enduring aspect of the women's equality movement. During the 1800s, the very choice of wearing bloomers rather than skirts or dresses was a political statement.

This song focuses on the impact of Eliza Jane's bicycle-riding and bloomer-wearing on those around her, claiming that her actions cause her brothers to become drunkards, her fiancé to scream and flee, dogs to bark, and ultimately causing all around to "have a pain" when they see her.

"Eliza Jane" describes not only the shame that the "Twentieth Century Girl" brings to her family, but also states that such a woman is masculine ("Eliza plans to be a man"), will never find a husband, and even that she will wind up in a mental institution ("Asylums yawn for you, my dear, and in the books we read, / How bloomers that too early bloom soon fade and go to seed."). A woman's outward appearance has long been perceived as a reflection of her inner self: from the suffragists' choice to wear white to the modern struggle of women to wear or not wear a hijab. Indeed, the various backlashes against changing standards of women's dress provides insight into the way women are kept "in their place," even as they strive for an equal place in society. From the fight to ride a bike in the U.S. in 1895, to the fight to drive a car in Saudi Arabia in 2019, women continue to campaign for their freedom of movement.

Susan B. Anthony famously opined: "I think [the bicycle] has done more to emancipate women than any one thing in the world. I rejoice every time I see a woman ride by on a wheel. It gives her a feeling of self-reliance and independence the moment she takes her seat; and away she goes, the picture of untrammeled womanhood."

Library of Congress, 1895.

Excerpt from "Eliza Jane"

Lyrics by Winthrop Packard
1895

Eliza Jane she had a wheel, its rim was painted red;
Eliza had another wheel that turned inside her head.
She put the two together, she gave them both a whirl,
And now she rides the Parkway sides a Twentieth Century Girl.

Refrain:
"Oh, have you seen Eliza Jane a-cycling in the park?"
"Oh, have you seen Eliza Jane?" The people all remark.
They shout "Hi! Hi!" as she rides by; the little doggies bark,
For we all have a pain when Eliza Jane goes cycling in the park.

This is emancipation year, the woman movement's on;
Eliza plans to be a man, 'tis sad to think upon.
She thinks she needs the ballot now her freedom to enhance,
She wants to pose in papa's clothes; it is for this she pants.

Refrain

Eliza had a nice young man, (Alas! 'twas long ago.)
As gay and fair, as debonair, as any man you know;
He saw her ride in bloomers, he screamed and quickly fled,
And as he ran, this nice young man in trembling accents said:

Refrain

Eliza's ma no longer speaks unto Eliza Jane,
She claims that dime museum freaks give her a sense of pain.
Her dad no longer cashes checks but wanders in the streets,
And thus he cries, in sad surprise, to everyone he meets:

Refrain

Eliza's brothers saw her ride, and each one took to drink:
They made it flow to drown their woe, so that they need not think;
But there are woes that will not drown, not even in a well,
And in the worst of their great thirst Eliza hears them yell:

…

Women repairing bicycle, 1895. (Picture Collection, Library Montana State University Bozeman)

"Three Blind Men"

SONGS RELATED TO SUFFRAGE WEREN'T thematically limited to arguments in favor of the cause; some even made fun of their opposition. For example, the song "Three Blind Men," set to the popular nursery rhyme tune, "Three Blind Mice," mocks men who feel threatened by suffrage: likening them to thieves, cowards, and liars.

"Three Blind Men" was published in *The Suffrage Song Book* along with twenty-seven other pro-suffrage songs set to popular music and written by Henry Roby, a prominent Kansas doctor who wrote and assisted in writing numerous books, including the *Diseases of Women*.

As with so many other suffragists, Dr. Roby's activism and support for women's rights has been left out of the historical narrative. Neither his entry in the *Who's Who in Topeka* nor his obituary in the *Topeka Daily State Journal* mention his role in the suffrage movement. Yet without the active support of people like Henry Roby, the Nineteenth Amendment would not have been passed.

"Three Blind Mice" illustration by Edmund Caldwell, 1887.
(University of Florida)

Songs of the Suffragists

"Three Blind Men"

Lyrics by Henry W. Roby
1909

Three blind men,
Three blind men,
See how they stare, see how they stare;
They each ran off with a woman's right.
And they each went blind in a single night.
Did you ever behold such a gruesome sight
As these blind men?

Three blind men,
Three blind men,
The man who won't, the man who can't,
And then the coward who dares not try;
They're not fit to live and not fit to die.
Did you ever see such a three-cornered lie
As these blind men?

"Three Blind Mice" illustration by Edmund Caldwell, 1887.
(University of Florida)

"The March of the Women"

WHILE THE SUFFRAGE MOVEMENT WAS underway in the United States, activists in the United Kingdom were also fighting for the vote. The Women's Social and Political Union, founded in 1903, was a U.K. organization that employed visible public protests and large parades in addition to more radical acts. Dame Ethel Smyth, a member of the WSPU, composed the song, "The March of the Women," which soon became the anthem of the suffragette movement in the U.K., and later around the world. In 1916, Alice Paul and Lucy Burns organized the National Women's Party in the U.S., employing many of the more visible and radical tactics of the WSPU.

The women of the WSPU did not sing "The March of the Women," but rather shouted it as they marched through the streets. This attitude is characteristic of the WSPU, which was known for its riotous approach to fighting for women's suffrage, epitomized by its motto: "Deeds, not words."

Led by Emmeline Pankhurst and her daughters, the WSPU, whose members were called "suffragettes," was founded in 1903, but ceased its activities in 1914 with the outbreak of World War I, and officially dissolved in 1917. The U.K. granted limited voting rights to women in 1918, and equalized the franchise in 1928.

The WSPU gained notoriety for its members' militant acts, including hunger strikes, stone-throwing and arson. Suffragettes chained themselves to railings outside Parliament, and broke the windows of politicians, which frequently resulted in their arrest and imprisonment. Imprisonment, however, did not end the WSPU's fight for the vote. In fact, Smyth's most famous performance of "The March of the Women" came from within the confines of Holloway Prison.

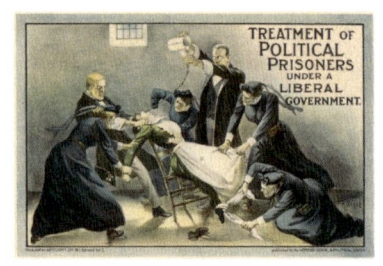

Imprisoned suffragette on hunger strike Being force-fed through the nose, 1910. (Mary Evans Picture Library)

Songs of the Suffragists

"The March of the Women"
Composed by Dame Ethel Smyth
Lyrics by Cicely Hamilton
1910

Shout, shout, up with your song!
Cry with the wind, for the dawn is breaking;
March, march, swing you along,
Wide blows our banner, and hope is waking.
Song with its story, dreams with their glory
Lo! they call, and glad is their word!
Loud and louder it swells,
Thunder of freedom, the voice of the Lord!

Long, long—we in the past
Cowered in dread from the light of heaven,
Strong, strong—stand we at last,
Fearless in faith and with sight new given.
Strength with its beauty, Life with its duty,

(Hear the voice, oh hear and obey!)
These, these—beckon us on!
Open your eyes to the blaze of day.

Comrades—ye who have dared
First in the battle to strive and sorrow!
Scorned, spurned—naught have ye cared,
Raising your eyes to a wider morrow,
Ways that are weary, days that are dreary,

Toil and pain by faith ye have borne;
Hail, hail—victors ye stand,
Wearing the wreath that the brave have worn!

Life, strife—those two are one,
Naught can ye win but by faith and daring.
On, on—that ye have done
But for the work of today preparing.
Firm in reliance, laugh a defiance,
(Laugh in hope, for sure is the end)
March, march—many as one,
Shoulder to shoulder and friend to friend.

Museum of London, 1911.

"How Can Such Things Be?"

Rally songs played a critical role in suffrage demonstrations. Unlike other pro-suffrage songs that were intended to be read, or which were dedicated to fellow suffragists and locally produced in small numbers, rally songs were set to popular music and printed on single-page leaflets. These songs united protesters at pro-suffrage demonstrations. Suffragists often faced significant opposition by counter-demonstrators and hecklers; rally songs helped unite protesters, as well as display their strength of numbers.

Prior to the Nineteenth Amendment, western states and territories were generally the first to grant women the right to vote, either with limited voting rights (*e.g.* to vote for president), or fully. When Congress objected to Wyoming's enfranchisement of women, the state telegrammed congressional leaders: "We will remain out of the Union one hundred years rather than come in without our women."

"How Can Such Things Be?" notes the fight for suffrage that was on-going in the states at this time. The first lines are: "I came from California, where the women folk are free, / I'm bound for Pennsylvania, old-fashioned folks to see!" California granted women suffrage in 1911, and in 1914, when this song was written, suffragists were actively campaigning in Pennsylvania and the other eastern states shown in blue in the below map. The chorus of this song is similar to other pro-suffrage songs that link the issue of women's suffrage with freedom, asking how the U.S. can consider itself a free nation if "only one-half can be free?"

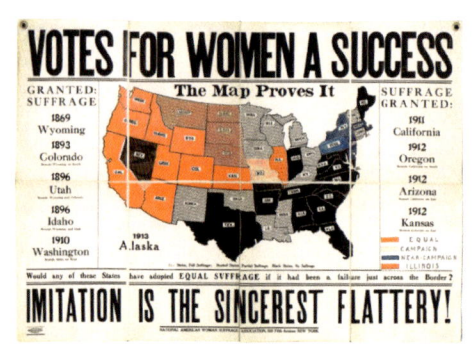

Map of women's suffrage support by state, 1914.
(Manuscript Division, Library of Congress)

Songs of the Suffragists

"How Can Such Things Be?"
Lyrics by Eugénie M. Rayé-Smith
Tune "Oh Susannah!"
1914

I came from California, where the women folk are free,
I'm bound for Pennsylvania, old-fashioned folks to see!
Election night the day I left and every poll all right;
I crossed the line, near lost my breath; election was a fight:

Chorus:
Oh, men voters,
How can such things be?
In all this free America
Only one-half can be free!

I traveled long, I traveled fast, I went by rail and river;
Election sights in many a state, they'd make a home man shiver!
Some men they say too decent are; they will not come to vote;
Says I, "Invite the women out and then a change you'll note!"

Then came a revelation when I neared my journey's end,
I saw the lowest ranks of men to polling places wend,
While wistfully some women gazed a block or two away
As to the assessor's door they passed their taxes for to pay!
If I could run for President, I'd want a good clean fight;
I'd want the women on my side, I'd grant their equal right;
I'd pledge my word of honor in the lists to meet them fair,
And if they asked me for a deal, I'd make it on the square.

"The Awakening" showing western states that granted women the right to vote, 1915. (Library of Congress)

"The Anti-Suffrage Rose"

SYMBOLS WERE IMPORTANT TO THE suffrage movement. Just as slogans, signs, cartoons, and songs helped underscore the arguments on both sides, both proponents and opponents of women's suffrage outwardly displayed their support through their attire. For example, suffragists favored white dresses, that would stand out while they marched, as well as yellow for their banners, clothing, and flowers. The jonquil (or daffodil), along with yellow roses and paper yellow chrysanthemums were worn by suffragists. Both male and female suffragists sported yellow flowers to signify their support for extending the franchise to women. Suffrage opponents soon countered by adopting the red rose as their own symbol. During legislative debates over the Nineteenth Amendment, members of Congress donned boutonnieres of yellow and red roses to show which side they supported.

Famously, Tennessee became the thirty-sixth state to ratify the Nineteenth Amendment, when on August 18, 1920, Harry Burn cast his vote in favor, while still wearing the red boutonniere signifying his opposition. At the last minute, he changed his mind (and his intended vote) after receiving a letter from his mother encouraging him to vote in favor of suffrage.

"The Anti-Suffrage Rose" by Phil Hanna was intended to broadcast and popularize the red rose as a symbol of the opposition. This song is more of a rallying cry for people already convinced of the rightness of their cause, as opposed to a song intended to persuade listeners. It does not cite specific reasons for why women should not vote, simply highlighting the beauty of a "lovely red, red rose," and implying that the anti-suffragists were more popular than the few supporters of suffrage ("Why should a few / Rule over you?").

Library of Congress, 1911.

Songs of the Suffragists

"The Anti-Suffrage Rose"
Music and Lyrics by Phil Hanna
1915

Suffragists say
Happen what may
They'll win the coming fight
'Twixt you and me
I don't agree
We're going to show them who's right!

Jonquils they wear
Cannot compare
With the Anti-Suffrage Rose
Token of love
And a gift from above
Loveliest flow'r that grows

Red, red, Anti-Suffrage Rose
You're the flow'r that's best of all!
You're better far, that Jonquils are
We are going to prove it in the Fall
Sweetest flow'r in all the world
Ev'ry body knows
You're the emblem of the
    Anti-Suffrage Cause
You lovely, red, red rose!

Work for the "cause"
No time to pause
Tell all the men you know
Why should a few
Rule over you?

Suffrage is ev'ry man's foe
Beautiful flower
Sign of the hour
If the Jonquil wants to fight
You cannot fall
You're the Queen of them all
Emblem of Truth and Right

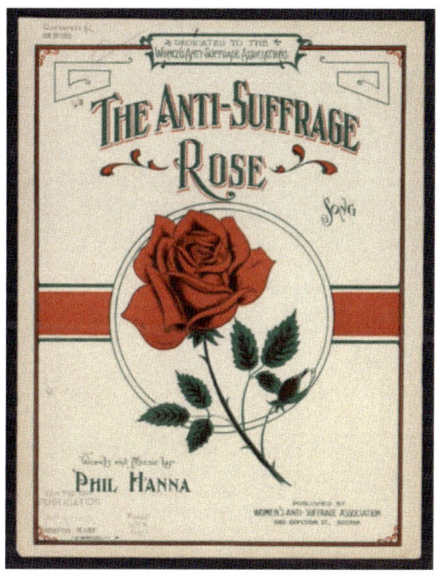

Library of Congress, Music Division, 1915.

"She's Good Enough to Be Your Baby's Mother"

IN 1916, THE SUFFRAGE MOVEMENT gained momentum when President Woodrow Wilson declared the Democratic Party's support for women's suffrage. This year also marked the first election of a woman to federal office, when Jeannette Rankin was elected to represent Montana in the House of Representatives. As the United States mobilized and fought World War I, the country's need for women to broaden their participation in society beyond the confines of their homes became increasingly obvious.

In 1918, Representative Rankin introduced the Nineteenth Amendment, the text of which remained practically identical to that first proposed in 1868 and again in 1914. This time however, the amendment passed the House and went onto the Senate, where Woodrow Wilson made a direct address in favor of its passage, arguing that it was unjust to rely on women in the war effort, while denying them the franchise. Despite President Wilson's support, the bill failed in the Senate and it would be another year before Congress ultimately passed the amendment.

In 1919, the Nineteenth Amendment was finally approved by both the House and the Senate, and went on to be ratified by the state legislatures. On August 18, 1920, Tennessee became the thirty-sixth and final state needed to ratify the amendment. On August 26, now celebrated in this country as Women's Equality Day, the Nineteenth Amendment became part of the Constitution.

The song "She's Good Enough to Be Your Baby's Mother and She's Good Enough to Vote with You" highlighted one persuasive argument for women's suffrage — if we believe women are capable of raising children, how can we believe them incapable of voting? Women do indeed have the knowledge and intelligence to vote, and at last in 1920, the United States recognized that.

Representative Jeannette Rankin speaking from the balcony of the National Woman Suffrage Association, 1917. (Library of Congress)

Songs of the Suffragists

"She's Good Enough to Be Your Baby's Mother And She's Good Enough to Vote with You"

Music by Herman Paley

Lyrics by Alfred Bryan

1916

No man is greater than his mother
No man is half so good
No man is better than the wife he loves
Her love will guide him
What 'ere beguile him

She's good enough to love you and
    adore you
She's good enough to bear your
    troubles for you
And if your tears were falling today
Nobody else would kiss them away
She's good enough to warm your heart
    with kisses
When your lonesome and blue
She's good enough to be your baby's
    mother
And she's good enough to vote with you

Man plugs the world in war and sadness
She must protest in vain
Let's hope and pray someday we'll hear
    her pain
Stop all your madness, I bring you
    gladness

She's good enough to love you and
    adore you
She's good enough to bear your
    troubles for you
And if your tears were falling today
Nobody else would kiss them away
She's good enough to warm your heart
    with kisses

When your lonesome and blue She's good
    enough to be your baby's mother
And she's good enough to vote with you

She's good enough to give you old
    Abe Lincoln
She good enough to give you
    Brandon Sherman
Robert E. Lee and Washington too
She was so true she gave them to you
She's good enough to give you
    Teddy Roosevelt
Thomas A. Edison too.
She's good enough to give you
    Woodrow Wilson
And she's good enough to vote with
    you.

Library of Congress, Music Division.

Songs of the Suffragists

Suffragists picketing outside the White House, 1917. (Associated Press)

The Suffragist was the "official weekly organ of the National Women's Party" to educate the public on women's suffrage and gain support. It dissolved after the passing of the Nineteenth Amendment, 1919. (National Museum of American History, Smithsonian Institute)

26

Songs of the Suffragists

Alice Paul raising a toast (of grape juice) to the passage of the Nineteenth Amendment, 1920. (Library of Congress)

Women casting ballots, ca. 1920. (Library of Congress)

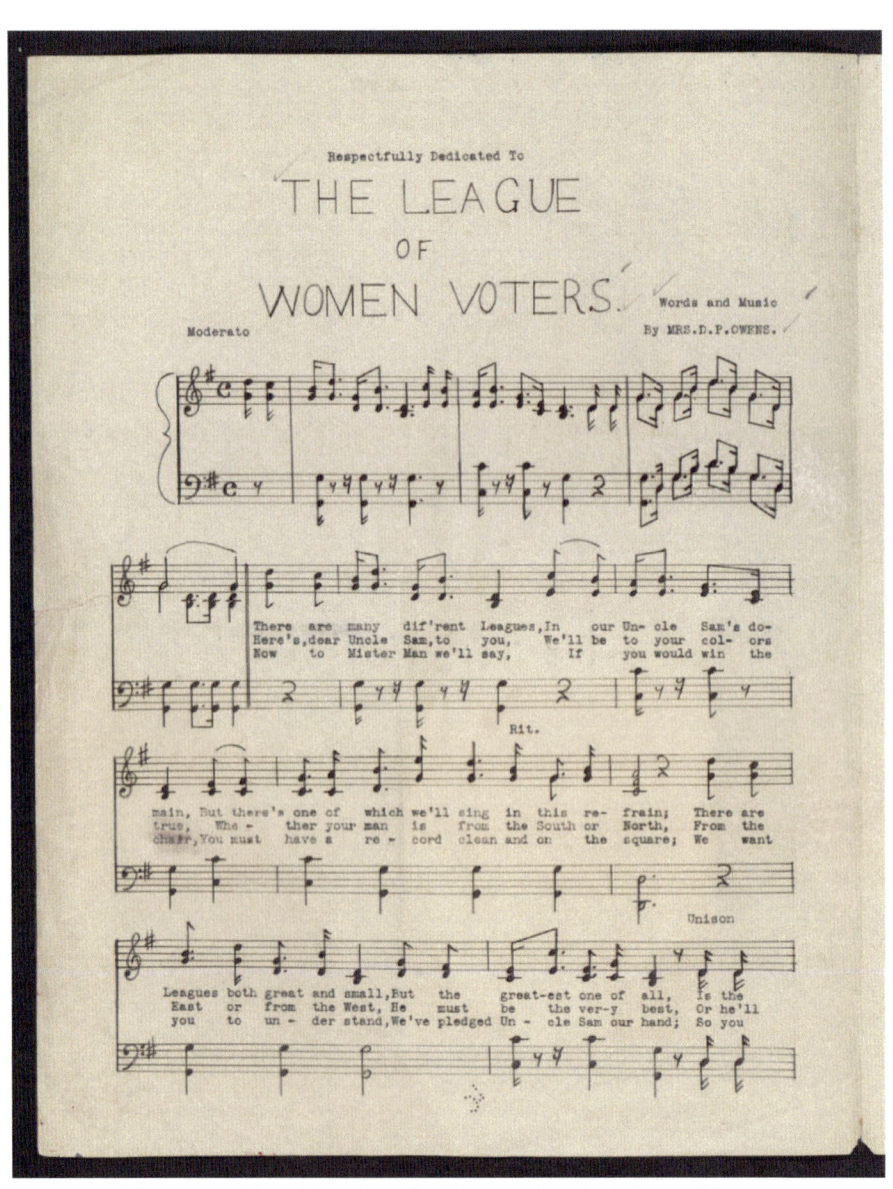

The League of Women Voters: Song. © 1923 Notated Music. (Library of Congress)

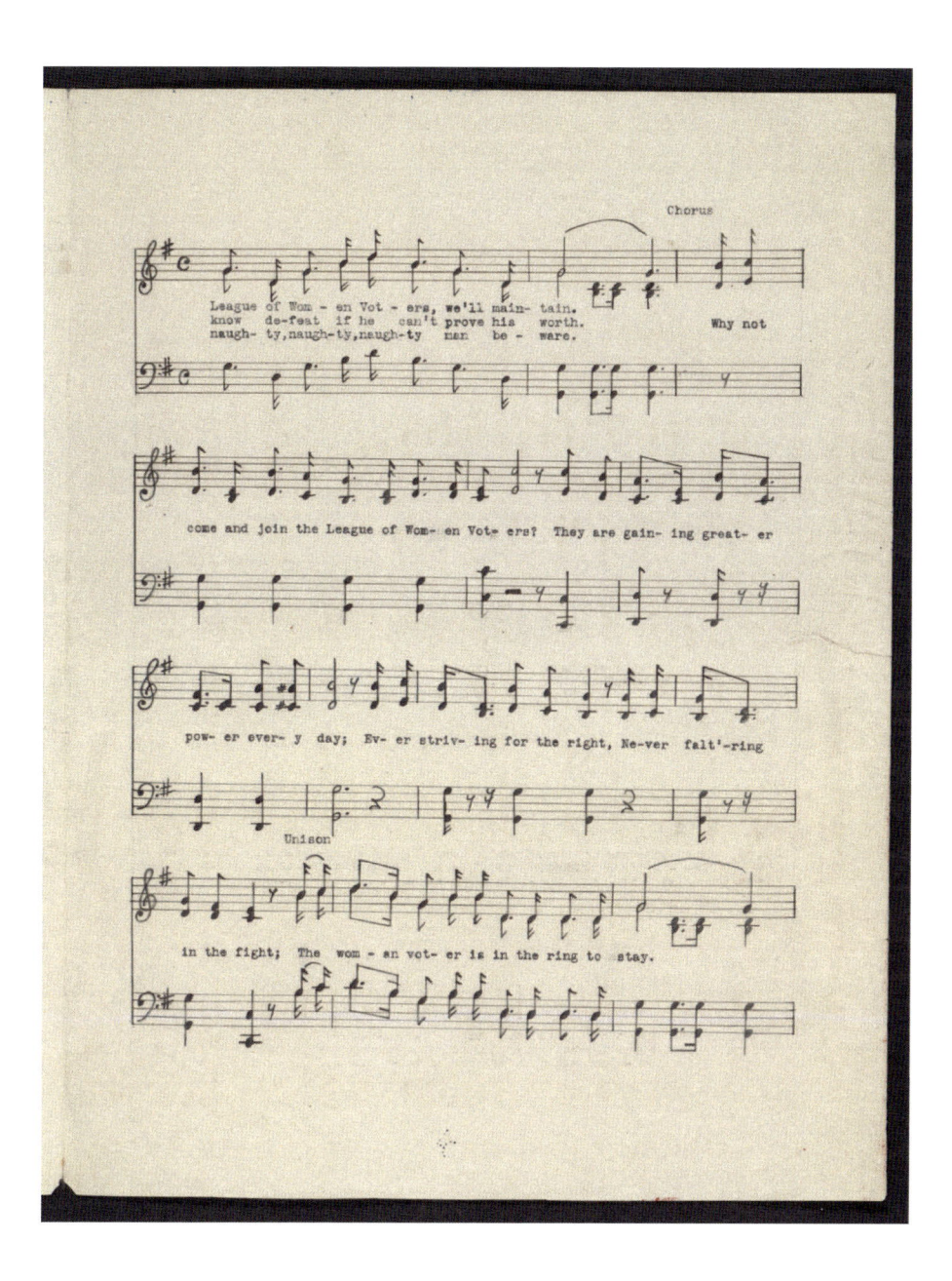

Songs of the Suffragists

"Rosie the Riveter"

WHILE WOMEN GAINED THE VOTE in 1920, the fight to achieve true political and social equality for women was far from over. Well after the Nineteenth Amendment was ratified, many of the same arguments against women's suffrage remained part of the public discourse, continuing to shape the public's views of women and restricting women's lives.

Yet the onset of World War II marked another period of social change, as women again met the demands of wartime by stepping out of their traditional roles in dramatic fashion. During the 1940s, the country's wartime personnel needs forced a large number of women out of the domestic sphere to take the jobs vacated by men serving in the armed forces.

"We Can Do It!" voiced Rosie the Riveter, representative of the new woman of the WWII-era. This poster has become a cultural emblem, and an enduring symbol of the feminist movement. While many today are familiar with the iconic image, few are aware that the original Rosie the Riveter was a character in a song.

The song, "Rosie the Riveter," highlights the crucial contributions of women to the war, and was written to inspire women to leave their homes and join the workforce. Its intent was to combat the stereotypes popular from the anti-suffrage days: that women who left their traditional sphere were unfeminine embarrassments, who would be unable to find a husband, would drive their brothers to drink, and ultimately wind up in an institution (*see* "Eliza Jane").

During the 1940s, this song was recorded by numerous artists, becoming a national hit. While singers of more common wartime hits warble of men's heroism or of a sweetheart waiting at home for her man's safe return, "Rosie the Riveter" flips the script: "Rosie is protecting Charlie," the Marine, by "working overtime on the riveting machine."

World War II expanded the cultural vision of women's roles, and declarations of equality began to permeate the international political sphere. In 1945, the United Nations Charter was signed in San Francisco, providing that: "We the peoples of the United Nations … reaffirm faith … in the equal rights of men and women …" However, U.S. society was still not ready to for gender equality. For example, it wasn't until the 1970s that state laws forbidding women from holding credit cards and serving on juries were overturned. In fact, the right to vote is the only right explicitly extended to both men and women in the U.S. Constitution.

Songs of the Suffragists

Excerpt from **"Rosie the Riveter"**
Music and Lyrics by Redd Evans and John Jacob Loeb
1942

While other girls attend their fav'rite
 cocktail bar
Sipping Martinis, munching caviar
There's a girl who's really putting
 them to shame
Rosie is her name

All the day long whether rain or shine
She's a part of the assembly line
She's making history,
working for victory
Rosie the Riveter
Keeps a sharp lookout for sabotage
Sitting up there on the fuselage
That little frail can do more than a
 male will do
Rosie the Riveter

Rosie's got a boyfriend, Charlie
Charlie, he's a Marine
Rosie is protecting Charlie
Working overtime on the riveting
 machine
When they gave her a production "E"
She was as proud as a girl could be
There's something true about
Red, white, and blue about
Rosie the Riveter

...

Rosie the Riveter, 1942. (National Museum of American History, Smithsonian Institution)

Songs of the Suffragists

"You Don't Own Me"

THE PASSAGE OF THE NINETEENTH Amendment was a critical first step towards achieving political equality for women, but this was only the start of the movement towards equal rights. The so-called "second wave" of feminism began in the 1960s, as activists shifted their focus from achieving political equality towards a more holistic focus on the experience of women in society, including politics, work, the family, and sexuality. Phrases such as "the personal is political" and "identity politics" entered the cultural lexicon, highlighting how individual struggles were indicative of greater socio-cultural issues intertwined within political structures.

Emblematic of this new era of feminism is Lesley Gore's "You Don't Own Me." Gore defiantly sings that she is "free" and not owned by her boyfriend. This was — and still is — a powerful message, as women's bodies, minds and even spirits are perceived as rightfully controlled by the men in their lives. The existence of normalized control by men over "their" women is critical to "the personal is political" ideology that characterized feminism during the 1960s and '70s. This 1963 message of personal independence is reprised in the 2017 song "Woman," where the emphasis is on economic independence. Gore's demand to be free to do as she chooses also reminds us of the 1851 bloomer who sang of her indifference to men's scorn and ridicule, claiming she was determined to wear bloomers if "only to spite them," and foreshadows the 2017 song, "Hijab," where "even if you hate it / I still wrap my hijab."

Gore's song resonated with the American public, and it was a commercial success, peaking at #2 on the *Billboard* Hot 100 in 1964. Additionally, the song has since been covered by numerous artists and most recently by Grace and featuring G-Eazy in 2016, who put a more modern spin on the song, while still conveying the same ever-relevant message.

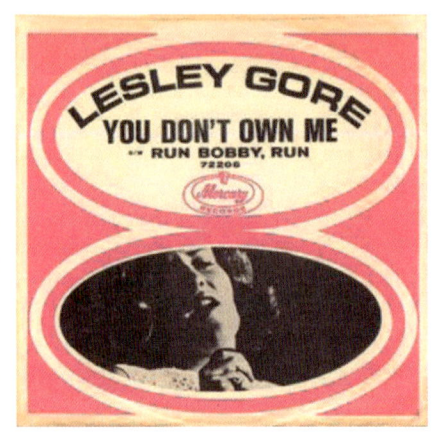

Cover for the 7" single of "You Don't Own Me," 1963. (Mercury Records)

Songs of the Suffragists

Excerpt from **"You Don't Own Me"**
Written by John Madara and David White
Recorded by Lesley Gore
1963

You don't own me
I'm not just one of your many toys
You don't own me
Don't say I can't go with other boys

Chorus:
And don't tell me what to do
Don't tell me what to say
And please, when I go out with you
Don't put me on display 'cause

You don't own me
Don't try to change me in any way
You don't own me
Don't tie me down 'cause I'd never stay

…

Post-Chorus:
I'm young, and I love to be young
I'm free, and I love to be free
To live my life the way I want
To say and do whatever I please

Lesley Gore performing "You Don't Own Me" in 1964.

"Four Women"

IN 1966, NINA SIMONE RECORDED the song, "Four Women." The lyrics are characteristic of the new rallying cry that "the personal is political" and is emblematic of the new form of "identity politics," as the movements for racial and gender equality intersect in this song. "Four Women" is structured in four verses, each narrating a portrait of a different African American woman, and each representing a different archetype of the black female experience throughout our history. The song begins quietly, with a driving beat. Nina Simone's voice escalates in ferocity and emotion until the song reaches its screaming climax.

The first verse is sung by Aunt Sarah, representing the first generation of enslaved African American women. The next verse is sung by Saffronia, a mixed-race woman conceived by a rich white man's rape of her black mother. This verse underscores slavery's legacy, and the power structure supporting rich white men. The third verse describes a prostitute called, "Sweet Thing," whose profession allows her to be possessed ("Whose little girl am I? / Anyone who has money to buy"). The final and most intense persona is Peaches, a woman made angry enough to kill because of the generations of dehumanization African Americans have experienced. She ends the song by reclaiming her identity as she cries, "My name is Peaches!"

The song evokes many different emotions: validation for some, discomfort and offense in others. But songs whose purpose is to force change should not make one feel comfortable or content, they are a call to action. Music was Nina Simone's medium for change. Like the women of the WSPU who shouted "The March of the Women" as they protested in the streets, Nina Simone's song opposing oppression and suffering is raw, powerful, and disconcerting.

"Four Women" has transcended its time, and has been reused by artists over the years, similar to how the "Battle Hymn of the Republic" was leveraged to align the morality of the suffrage movement with the moral underpinnings of abolitionism. In 2017, the rap artist Jay-Z used a sample from "Four Women" in his 2017 hit, "The Story of O.J.," to stress his vehement disagreement with O.J. Simpson's famous claim: "I'm not black, I'm O.J." Jagged excerpts from Simone's iconic song play beneath Jay-Z's entire rap to underscore his view that color blindness is impossible. Jay-Z sampled "Four Women" in his song to support his view that, for African Americans, no amount of fame or fortune can erase the legacy of slavery and its multi-generational impact.

Excerpt from **"Four Women"**
Written and recording by Nina Simone
1966

My skin is black
My arms are long
My hair is woolly
My back is strong
Strong enough to take the pain
Inflicted again and again
What do they call me?
My name is Aunt Sarah
My name is Aunt Sarah
Aunt Sarah

…

My skin is brown
My manner is tough
I'll kill the first mother I see!
My life has been rough
I'm awfully bitter these days
Because my parents were slaves
What do they call me?
My name is Peaches!

Nina Simone singing "Four Women" in Paris in 1961.

"Respect" and "I Am Woman"

IN 1965, OTIS REDDING WROTE a song about a man who gives a woman money, but does not receive respect from the woman in return. He does not care about what she does, so long as he is respected, as he says, "all I'm askin' / is for a little respect / when you come home."

In 1967, Aretha Franklin sung a song of women's liberation, a song about a woman demanding the respect she deserves from a man. Franklin's version of "Respect" uses Redding's lyrics (with a few tweaks) to convey a completely different message than the original. Franklin's message rang true for so many women, and presages the importance of the movement for the Equal Rights Amendment that occupied the 1970s.

Aretha Franklin performing "Respect" in 1968.

The ERA is a constitutional amendment that guarantees equal rights for all Americans, regardless of sex. First proposed by Alice Paul in 1923, Congress passed the amendment in 1972, establishing a 1979 deadline for state ratification. Only thirty-five states ratified it by the deadline, largely due to the advocacy of anti-feminist Phyllis Schlafly, who argued that the ERA would harm housewives. Five states even rescinded their ratification! Nevertheless, activists persist in seeking state approval. In 2020, Virginia ratified the ERA, becoming the thirty-eighth and final state necessary for the amendment to become law, but for the legal uncertainty around state revocation of their ratification and the missed Congressional deadline.

The ERA was critical to second wave feminism, as it arguably embodied all that the women's liberation movement fought for. The anthem to this movement was "I Am Woman" by Helen Reddy. The song was uplifting, but fierce, speaking of the strength of women. Yet, "I Am Woman" would not have had such success if not for the support of a man — Reddy's husband, Jeff Wald — who pushed for its recording. Capitol Records told him that this "'women's lib crap is gonna kill her'" and "end her career." Wald responded by peeing on the desk at Capitol Records.

The song that was supposed to end Reddy's career, ended up *making* her career. Topping charts worldwide, including the peaking at #1 on the *Billboard* Hot 100, the song went on to win a Grammy. In her thank you speech Reddy thanked her husband, and God, "because *she* makes everything possible" (emphasis added).

Songs of the Suffragists

Excerpt from **"Respect"**
Written by Otis Redding
Recorded by Aretha Franklin
1965 (Redding)/1967 (Franklin)

What you want
Baby, I got it
What you need
Do you know I got it?

All I'm askin'
Is for a little respect
When you come home
(just a little bit)
Hey, baby
(just a little bit)

When you get home
(just a little bit)
Mister
(just a little bit)

…

R-E-S-P-E-C-T
Find out what it means to me
R-E-S-P-E-C-T
Take care, TCB

Excerpt from "I Am Woman"
Written by Ray Burton and Helen Reddy
Recorded by Helen Reddy
1972

I am woman, hear me roar
In numbers too big to ignore
And I know too much to go back and pretend
'Cause I've heard it all before
And I've been down there on the floor
No one's ever going to keep me down again

…

Oh, I am woman
I am invincible
I am strong
I am woman
I am invincible
I am strong
I am woman

Helen Reddy performing "I Am Woman" in concert in 1971.

"The Pill"

TWO LANDMARK SUPREME COURT CASES revolutionized reproductive health care for women in the United States. The first was *Griswold v. Connecticut* in 1965, which ruled that under the Fourteenth Amendment, the Constitution protects marital privacy against state restrictions on the use of contraception. The second case was *Roe v. Wade* in 1973, which ruled that the right to abortion was similarly constitutionally protected.

Roe opened a national debate and movements on both sides — pro-choice and anti-abortion. Both groups claim the moral high ground: pro-choice activists arguing for a woman's right to own and control her own body, and pro-life activists for an embryo/fetus' right to be born. The ability of women to control their bodies, and competing claims of ownership has been a defining political issue openly debated since the 1970s.

In 1975, Loretta Lynn released "The Pill," a country song of women's reproductive freedom that was met with both acclaim and denunciation. The song is about a mother who has become liberated from constant childbearing thanks to the pill. Lynn herself had six children (three before she was twenty years old), and once said: "If I'd had the pill back when I was havin' babies I'd have taken 'em like popcorn."

Due to the subject of the song and the more conservative views held by purveyors of country music in particular, the song was banned from numerous radio stations. Nevertheless, "The Pill" still charted at #70 on the *Billboard* Hot 100 and #5 on the country singles rankings.

Despite the music industry's resistance to the song, "The Pill" had a huge impact on normalizing the use of oral contraceptives in the United States. In an interview with *Playgirl* magazine, Lynn spoke of how doctors had commended her because they believed her song had done more to persuade rural Americans to accept and embrace the use of contraceptives than the medical sector or social service organizations.

A 1972 *60 Minutes* segment explores the abortion debate, showing footage of pro-choice women marching.

Songs of the Suffragists

Excerpt from **"The Pill"**
Written by Lorene Allen, Don McHan, T. D. Bayless, and Loretta Lynn
Recorded by Loretta Lynn
1975

You wined me and dined me when I was your girl
Promised if I'd be your wife
You'd show me the world
But all I've seen of this old world is a bed and a doctor bill
I'm tearing down your brooder house
'Cause now I've got the pill

All these years I've stayed at home
While you had all your fun
And every year that's gone by
Another baby's come
There's gonna be some changes
Made right here on Nursery Hill
You've set this chicken your last time
'Cause now I've got the pill

This old maternity dress I've got
Is going in the garbage
The clothes I'm wearing from now on
Won't take up so much yardage
Miniskirts, hotpants and a few little fancy frills
Yeah, I'm making up for all those years since I've got the pill

…

It's getting dark
It's roosting time
Tonight's too good to be real
Aw, but Daddy don't you worry none
'Cause Mama's got the pill
Oh, Daddy don't you worry none
'Cause Mama's got the pill

Loretta Lynn performing "One's on the Way," another song about the role of women in motherhood, and "The Pill" in concert in 1985.

"Standing on the Shoulders" and "Rebel Girl"

FOR THE 75TH ANNIVERSARY OF the Nineteenth Amendment, a celebration was held in Washington, D.C., where "Standing on the Shoulders" was performed live. The song harkens back to the women who laid the foundation in the fight for women's rights as an inspiration for the continued fight for equality. The song is soft, and intended to instill a sense of history and pride in listeners for the feminist movement.

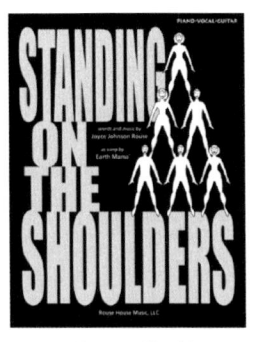

Joyce J. Rousse © 1995 Rouse House LLC (ASCAP). Used by Permission. All rights reserved.

The song, "Rebel Girl" by Bikini Kill, has a much different tone, yet is similarly intended to inspire women to activism. Within the 1990s grunge music genre, the riot grrrl subgenre of punk-powered feminism challenged double standards, sexual violence, and sexism. During concerts, riot grrrl bands often invited audience members to speak about their personal experiences, and demanded male audience members make space at the front for female concert-goers. Riot grrrl epitomized the fierceness characteristic of third wave feminism, as it sought to deconstruct conventional womanhood and the oppressive patriarchy.

Considered the anthem of riot grrrl, "Rebel Girl" admires girls who don't follow the rules of patriarchy — girls who are revolutionary are "queen." The sound is raw, even angry — an emotion women are often criticized for expressing. To characterize a woman or her argument as "angry," is to dismiss her without further need to counter her claims. While male anger is often interpreted as a marker of power and authority, an "angry woman" is ridiculed as hormonal or crazy. Riot grrrl music was characterized by its challenge to such gendered norms.

"Rebel Girl," aptly produced by punk rock icon Joan Jett, received critical acclaim. While Bikini Kill never topped the charts, their music and band members were highly influential in the punk music scene. For instance, Nirvana's single, "Smells Like Teen Spirit," was inspired by a message Bikini Kill frontwoman, Kathleen Hanna, wrote on Kurt Cobain's door: "Kurt smells like Teen Spirit." Unaware that Hanna was referring to the deodorant her fellow band member wore, Cobain found the phrase revolutionary, using it as the title for one of the band's greatest hits.

Excerpt from **"Standing on the Shoulders"**
Written by Joyce Rouse
1995

I am standing on the shoulders of the ones who came before me
I am stronger for their courage, I am wiser for their words
I am lifted by their longing for a fair and brighter future
I am grateful for their vision, for their toiling on this Earth

We are standing on the shoulders of the ones who came before us
They are saints and they are humans, they are angels, they are friends
We can see beyond the struggles and the troubles and the challenge
When we know that by our efforts things will be better in the end
…
I am standing on the shoulders of the ones who came before me
I am honored by their passion for our liberty
I will stand a little taller, I will work a little longer
And my shoulders will be there to hold the ones who follow me

Excerpt from **"Rebel Girl"**
Written and recorded by Kathleen Hanna, Billy Karren, Tobi Vail, and Kathi Wilcox (Bikini Kill)
1993

That girl thinks she's the queen of the neighborhood
She's got the hottest trike in town
That girl, she holds her head up so high
I think I wanna be her best friend, yeah

Rebel girl, rebel girl
Rebel girl you are the queen of my world
Rebel girl, rebel girl
I think I wanna take you home
I wanna try on your clothes, uh

Kathleen Hanna performing "Rebel Girl" with Bikini Kill.

When she talks, I hear the revolution
In her hips, there's revolution
When she walks, the revolution's coming
In her kiss, I taste the revolution

Songs of the Suffragists

"Hijabi"

FROM THE 1850S TO THE 1890s, activists in the "rational dress movement" sought to free white, upper-class women from the restrictive, and even physically damaging fashions of the time. The rise of bloomers stirred a backlash, where many characterized women who wore "sensible" attire as unfeminine and even crazy. Women's outward appearance has long been seen as a sign of conformity or nonconformity to prevailing expectations of women's roles. The personal remains political, now, as it did then.

A growing backlash against school dress codes has been gathering force since the 2010s, with opponents arguing that they have been disproportionately used against girls, particularly girls of color, who are publicly shamed and sent home from for wearing attire seen as "distracting" to boys. On the other side of the skin-showing spectrum, hijab-wearing women have faced increasing discrimination since 9/11 for their choice to cover their heads and faces.

The intersection of feminism, patriarchy and religious discrimination encapsulated in the hijab is notable: from countries like the United States, where wearing a headscarf is a choice, to countries like France, where it is legally restricted, and others like Iran, where it is required. Each of these cultures is unique in their legal and cultural expectations towards women, and their expectations are reflected in both their laws and their social pressure regarding women's choice of dress.

Women in New Zealand wearing the hijab after the Christchurch shooting, 2019. (Channel 1 News, TVNZ.)

In the post-9/11 world, women have worn hijabs as protest against anti-Muslim sentiment (for example, after the 2019 mosque shootings in Christchurch, New Zealand woman donned hijabs for a day in solidarity with the victims and in protest against anti-Islamic terrorism). Mona Haydar wrote her song, "Hijabi," with the hope of empowering Muslim-American girls to feel visible and proud of who they are, as well as to protest the discrimination she experienced in U.S. airports.

Excerpt from "Hijabi (Wrap my Hijab)"

Music and Lyrics by Mona Haydar

2017

What that hair look like
Bet that hair look nice
Don't that make you sweat?
Don't that feel too tight?
Yo what yo hair look like
Bet yo hair look nice
How long your hair is
You need to get yo life
You only see Oriental
You steady working that dental
You poppin off at the lip
And run ya mouth like a treadmill
Not your exotic vacation
I'm bored with your fascination
I need that PayPal, PayPal, PayPal
If you want education
All around the world
Love women every shading
be so liberated
All around the world
Love women every shading
power run deep
So even if you hate it
…

I still wrap my hijab
Wrap my hijab
Wrap my hijab
Wrap, wrap my hijab
Keep swaggin my hijabis
Swag-Swaggin my hijabis
Swaggin my hijabis
Swag-swaggin my hijabis
Me and my hijabi ladies
We was born in the eighties
So pretty like the euphrates
and party like some kuwaitis
Deeper than some diplomas
Current like some hot yoga
Takin back the misnomers and
Teleportin through trauma
Teleportin through trauma
Teleportin through trauma
I been stackin my karma
Nefertiti, no drama
Make a feminist planet
Women haters get banished
Covered up or not don't ever
    take us for granted
…

Mona Haydar (center) in the "Hijabi" music video.

Songs of the Suffragists

"Woman"

When looking at the history of feminism, there is one common theme: women rising. Women rising despite not having the right to vote. Women rising to gain the right to vote. Women rising for reproductive freedom. Women rising for control of their own bodies. Women rising for women who cannot. Women rising, despite society systematically putting them down.

Still today, women rise. A major part of modern feminism is the Me Too movement, where women are speaking out and rising up against sexual harassment and sexual assault. In 2014, the popstar Kesha sued producer Dr. Luke for sexual, physical, verbal, and emotional abuse. Her case was complicated by her contract, which required her to continue to make music with her alleged abuser under his record label Kemosabe Records (a Sony subsidiary). Eventually, Kesha worked out a deal with Sony: while still required to produce her album under Kemosabe's label, she was no longer required to work with Dr. Luke personally. Her third album, *Rainbow*, was released after Kesha's new agreement with Sony. The *Kesha v. Dr. Luke* lawsuit is emblematic of the challenges faced by individual women, even rich and famous women, in demanding a workplace free of sexual violence.

Actress Alyssa Milano's original October 15, 2017 tweet that sparked the Me Too movement.

Rainbow departs from the electropop, club music style of Kesha's two previous albums. The songs on *Rainbow* merge musical styles: from pop dance music to ballads and songs with country twang, featuring themes of empowerment, forgiveness and strength. The album showcases Kesha's vocal range, songwriting capabilities and talent.

"Woman" is a song of female empowerment, written in protest against President Trump's pussy-grabbing comment that came out during the 2016 election cycle. The song celebrates women as standing proud and independent. Women are often abused, discriminated against, and put down simply because of their gender. Kesha's song channels the strength and power of an independent woman: it calls for us to rise, as she did.

Songs of the Suffragists

Excerpt from **"Woman"**
Written by Andrew Pearson, Kesha Sebert, and Stephen Wrabel
2017

Let's be serious, it's a real
This is, excuse me?
Ok, shut up

I buy my own things, I pay my own bills
These diamond rings, my automobiles
Everything I got, I bought it
Boys can't buy my love, buy my love, yeah

I do what I want (he does)
Say what you say
I work real hard every day

I'm a motherf---ing woman, baby, alright
I don't need a man to be holding me too tight
I'm a motherf---ing woman, baby, that's right
I'm just having fun with my ladies here tonight
I'm a motherf---er

...

Kesha performing in the music video of "Woman," 2017. (Kemosabe Records)

Postlude

SUFFRAGISTS WERE ACTIVISTS FOR WOMEN'S rights, first and foremost. In 1920, the right to vote was seen as a crucial step forward, but few saw it as the final step. Suffragists believed in the morality of their cause: that women were equal to men, and that achieving political equality was crucial to achieving greater equality in other areas of their lives. They were right.

Without the right to vote, women would have never had the influence on politics or social culture that they have in this country today. We stand on the shoulders of those who came before us. And while women have made great strides towards the goal of full equality, there is much left to do. Montana, which elected the first woman to federal office in 1916, has not elected another woman to the House or Senate since Representative Rankin. Women ran for federal office in historically high numbers in 2018, but in 2019, women only held between twenty-three to twenty-nine percent of elected offices at a state-wide and federal level. Work remains to be done to fulfill the equitable vision of our country the suffragists proposed over a century ago.

Suffragists marching in Washington, D.C., 1913. (Library of Congress)

We need to be vigilant in protecting the rights we have gained, including the right to participate in free and fair elections. For example, New Jersey women *were* able to vote in state elections from 1776 until 1807, when they were disenfranchised by law. Nowadays, disenfranchisement is achieved through poll access restrictions, gerrymandering and disinformation campaigns rather than outright legal prohibitions on voting. It is up to us to safeguard our elections and protect our franchise. Let us be mindful of the lessons of our past: rights we have gained can be lost.

We cannot give up on the ratification of the Equal Rights Amendment and all it represents. Yet changing the law is merely the first step forward: only by changing cultural norms can such paper changes endure. Songs, books, cartoons and plays were the tools used by suffragists to sway popular opinion and to permanently change the prevailing cultural norms. The efforts of the original suffragists so transformed our society that we now wonder how anyone could have ever thought that women should *not* vote.

To continue our march towards full equality, we must write our own songs in support of equality in the mediums of our modern era: songs created for YouTube and memes for text messaging, TV shows and movies. Only if we continue to write our new songs of suffrage will the concept of gender equality be so ingrained in our culture that one hundred years from today people may likewise wonder how that notion could have ever been in doubt. "Daughters of Freedom! The Ballot be Yours."

Thousands march down Pennsylvania Avenue in Washington, D.C. after the inauguration of Donald Trump as president, 2017. (Reuters)

References

"The Bloomer's Complaint"
1. *The bloomer's complaint; A very pathetic song.* Philadelphia, PA: A. Fiot, 1851. Accessed August 5, 2019. https://library.duke.edu/digitalcollections/hasm_a7230/.
2. Boissoneault, Lorraine. "Amelia Bloomer Didn't Mean to Start a Fashion Revolution, But Her Name Became Synonymous With Trousers." Smithsonian. Last modified May 24, 2018. Accessed July 23, 2019. https://www.smithsonianmag.com/history/amelia-bloomer-didnt-mean-start-fashion-revolution-her-name-became-synonymous-trousers-180969164/.
3. Loshbaugh, Bonnie, ed. "The Bloomer's Complaint." Loshbaugh. Last modified 2018. Accessed August 5, 2019. http://www.loshbaugh.com/2018/05/the-bloomers-complaint/#.XUjDbZNKgxc.
4. McGee, Suzanne and Moore, Heidi. "Women's rights and their money: a timeline from Cleopatra to Lilly Ledbetter." The Guardian. August 11, 2014. Accessed November 25, 2019. https://www.theguardian.com/money/us-money-blog/2014/aug/11/women-rights-money-timeline-history.

"Battle Hymn of the Republic" and "Dare You Do It"
1. Clinton, Catherine. *Harriet Tubman: The Road to Freedom.* 2004, at 191.
2. "Julia Ward Howe Biography." Julia Ward Howe Biography. Accessed July 18, 2019. http://www.juliawardhowe.org/bio.htm
3. Marshall, Nicholas. "The Civil War Death Toll, Reconsidered." *The New York Times.* Last modified April 15, 2014. Accessed August 5, 2019. https://opinionator.blogs.nytimes.com/2014/04/15/the-civil-war-death-toll-reconsidered/.
4. Roby, Henry W. *The Suffrage Song Book.* Topeka, KS: Crane and Company, 1909. Accessed July 21, 2019. https://www.kansasmemory.org/item/204064.
5. Tierney, Dominic. "'The Battle Hymn of the Republic': America's Song of Itself." *The Atlantic.* Last modified November 4, 2010. Accessed August 5, 2019. https://www.theatlantic.com/entertainment/archive/2010/11/the-battle-hymn-of-the-republic-americas-song-of-itself/66070/.

"Human Equality" and "Daughters of Freedom! The Ballot Be Yours"

1. Christie, Edwin. *Daughters of Freedom! The Ballot Be Yours* Boston, MA: Oliver Ditson & Co., 1871. Accessed August 9, 2019. http://www.pdmusic.org/1800s/71doftbby.txt.
2. *Human Equality. By William Lloyd Garrison.* Image. American Song Sheets Library of Congress Rare Books and Special Collections. Library of Congress, Washington, DC. Accessed August 5, 2019. https://www.loc.gov/item/amss.as105600
3. Kish Sklar, Kathryn. "Temperance & Suffrage." PBS. Accessed July 19, 2019. https://www.pbs.org/kenburns/not-for-ourselves-alone/temperance-suffrage.
4. Livermore, Mary Ashton Rice, *The Story of My Life*, 1899.
5. "William Lloyd Garrison." National Women's History Museum. Accessed July 23, 2019. http://www.crusadeforthevote.org/garrison.

"Shall Women Vote?"

1. Boylen, Frank. Shall Women Vote., Monographic, 1881. Notated Music. Accessed August 5, 2019. https://www.loc.gov/item/sm1881.10757/.
2. The Congressional Record, Vol. 10, p. 380.
3. Drexler, Ken, and Mary Champagne. "19th Amendment to the U.S. Constitution: Primary Documents in American History." Library of Congress. Last modified June 5, 2019. Accessed July 22, 2019. https://guides.loc.gov/19th-amendment.
4. Estabrook, D. "Keep Woman In Her Sphere, song lyrics." Protest Song Lyrics. Accessed August 5, 2019. http://www.protestsonglyrics.net/Women_Feminism_Songs/Keep-Woman-Sphere.phtml.
5. Gordon, Ann. "Looking for a Right to Vote: Introducing the Nineteenth Amendment. Accessed December 13, 2019. https://www.nps.gov/articles/introducing-the-19th-amendment.htm.
6. "Shall Women Vote? Song lyrics." Protest Song Lyrics. Accessed August 5, 2019. http://www.protestsonglyrics.net/Women_Feminism_Songs/Shall-Women-Vote.phtml.
7. "Women and the Temperance Movement." DPLA. Accessed August 7, 2019. https://dp.la/primary-source-sets/women-and-the-temperance-movement.

"Three Blind Men"
1. Roby, Henry W. *The Suffrage Song Book*. Topeka, KS: Crane and Company, 1909. Accessed July 21, 2019. https://www.kansasmemory.org/item/204064.
2. Dr. Henry W. Roby. The Topeka Daily State Journal – Monday Evening, August 23, 1920. Accessed August 7, 2019. https://www.findagrave.com/memorial/14262020/henry-wesley-roby#view-photo=129214154.
3. "Dr. Henry Wesley Roby." Find a Grave. Accessed August 7, 2019. https://www.findagrave.com/memorial/14262020/henry-wesley-roby.

"Oh, Dear, What Can the Matter Be?"
1. Borland, Elizabeth. "Analysis: 'Oh, Dear, What Can the Matter Be?'" Women's Suffrage in the United States. Last modified December 15, 2006. Accessed July 26, 2019. https://owd.tcnj.edu/~borland/2006-suffrage2/analysis.htm.
2. "Oh, Dear! What Can the Matter Be?" Lyrics On Demand. Accessed July 26, 2019. https://www.lyricsondemand.com/miscellaneouslyrics/childsongslyrics/ohdearwhatcanthematterbelyrics.html.
3. "Oh, Dear, What Can the Matter Be? Song lyrics." Protest Song Lyrics. Accessed July 26, 2019. http://www.protestsonglyrics.net/Women_Feminism_Songs/What-can-the-Matter-Be.phtml.

"Eliza Jane"
1. Dawson, Louise. "How the bicycle became a symbol of women's emancipation. *The Guardian*. Last modified November 4, 2011. Accessed August 7, 2019. https://www.theguardian.com/environment/bike-blog/2011/nov/04/bicycle-symbol-womens-emancipation.
2. Lange, Allison. "National Association Opposed to Woman Suffrage." National Women's History Museum. Last modified October 22, 2015. Accessed August 7, 2019. https://www.npr.org/sections/npr-history-dept/2015/10/22/450221328/american-women-who-were-anti-suffragettes.
3. Neubert, Michael. "Eliza Jane - A Woman Cyclist of 1895." From Wheels to Bikes. Last modified October 22, 2016. Accessed August 7, 2019. http://wheelbike.blogspot.com/2016/10/eliza-jane-woman-cyclist-of-1895.html.

4. "Songs of Women's Suffrage." Library of Congress. Accessed August 7, 2019. https://www.loc.gov/item/ihas.200197395/.
5. Weeks, Linton. "American Women Who Were Anti-Suffragettes." NPR. Last modified October 22, 2015. Accessed July 19, 2019. https://www.npr.org/sections/npr-history-dept/2015/10/22/450221328/american-women-who-were-anti-suffragettes.

"The March of the Women"
1. Abromeit, Kathleen A. "Ethel Smyth, The Wreckers, and Sir Thomas Beecham," The Musical Quarterly 73, no. 2 (1989): 205-206, accessed May 21, 2019, https://www.jstor.org/stable/742066.
2. "Four empowering feminist anthems – from the suffragettes to the Spice Girls." BBC. Accessed May 21, 2019. https://www.bbc.co.uk/programmes/articles/41ZsB3ttLKF1k8f8l6rDNT6/four-empowering-feminist-anthems-from-the-suffragettes-to-the-spice-girls.
3. Manners Smith, Karen. "Women's Social and Political Union." In Encyclopedia Britannica. Last modified March 17, 2017. Accessed May 21, 2019. https://www.britannica.com/topic/Womens-Social-and-Political-Union.
4. "Words to The March of the Women." Sandscape Publications. Accessed August 7, 2019. http://www.sandscapepublications.com/intouch/march-words.html.

"The Anti-Suffrage Rose"
1. Cohen, Jennie. "The Mother Who Saved Suffrage: Passing the 19th Amendment." History. Entry posted August 16, 2010. Accessed August 5, 2019. https://www.history.com/news/the-mother-who-saved-suffrage-passing-the-19th-amendment.
2. Miller, Cait. "Polarizing Political Issues: The Anti-Suffrage Rose." Library of Congress (blog). Entry posted March 27, 2019. Accessed May 25, 2019. https://blogs.loc.gov/music/2019/03/polarizing-political-issues-the-anti-suffrage-rose/.
3. The New York Times (New York, USA). "The Anti-Suffrage Rose: Women Who Don't Want to Vote Have a New War Song." August 28, 1915. Accessed May 25, 2019. https://timesmachine.nytimes.com/timesmachine/1915/08/28/100175102.html?pageNumber=7.

"How Can Such Things Be"
1. Klein, Christopher, "The State Where Women Voted Long Before the 19th Amendment." History. April 1, 2019. Accessed August 9, 2019. https://www.history.com/news/the-state-where-women-voted-long-before-the-19th-amendment.
2. Rayé-Smith, Eugénie M., -1914, Author, and Anna Howard Shaw. Equal Suffrage Song Sheaf. [Richmond Hill, New York City: Eugénie M. Rayé-Smith, ©, 1912] Image. https://www.loc.gov/item/2017562122/.
3. "Sheet Music." Woman Suffrage Memorabilia. Accessed July 28, 2019. http://womansuffragememorabilia.com/woman-suffrage-memorabilia/sheet-music/.
4. "States grant women the right to vote." National Constitution Center: Centuries of Citizenship: A Constitutional Timeline. Accessed July 27, 2019. https://constitutioncenter.org/timeline/html/cw08_12159.html.

"She's Good Enough to Be Your Baby's Mother and She's Good Enough to Vote with You"
1. A&E Television Networks. "President Woodrow Wilson speaks in favor of female suffrage." HISTORY. Last modified November 16, 2009. Accessed July 18, 2019. https://www.history.com/this-day-in-history/president-woodrow-wilson-speaks-in-favor-of-female-suffrage.
2. Ambar, Saladin. "Woodrow Wilson: Campaigns and Elections." Miller Center. Accessed July 18, 2019. https://millercenter.org/president/wilson/campaigns-and-elections.
3. Gordon, Ann. "Looking for a Right to Vote: Introducing the Nineteenth Amendment. Accessed December 13, 2019. https://www.nps.gov/articles/introducing-the-19th-amendment.htm.
4. "Sheet Music: She's Good Enough to Be Your Baby's Mother and She's Good Enough to Vote with You. Lyric by Alfred Bryan. Music by Herman Paley." Ann Lewis Women's Suffrage Collection. Accessed August 7, 2019. https://lewissuffragecollection.omeka.net/items/show/1306.
5. "Women in WWI." The National WWI Museum and Memorial. Accessed July 18, 2019. https://www.theworldwar.org/learn/women.

"Rosie the Riveter"
1. Dreher, Beth, "7 Shocking Things Women Weren't Allowed To Do Until Pretty Recently." Woman's Day, Aug 13, 2016. Accessed July 27, 2019. https://www.womansday.com/life/real-women/a55991/no-women-allowed/.
2. "Rosie the Riveter." Jacquelyn Whiting. Accessed July 18, 2019. http://jackiewhiting.net/US/RosieLyrics.html.
3. UN Charter. Accessed July 27, 2019. https://www.un.org/en/sections/un-charter/index.html.

"You Don't Own Me"
1. Burkett, Elinor. "Women's Rights Movement." In Encyclopædia Britannica. Encyclopædia Britannica, 2019. Last modified February 13, 2019. Accessed July 18, 2019. https://www.britannica.com/event/womens-movement.
2. Ulaby, Neda. "'You Don't Own Me,' A Feminist Anthem With Civil Rights Roots, Is All About Empathy." NPR. Last modified June 26, 2019. Accessed July 18, 2019. https://www.npr.org/2019/06/26/735819094/lesley-gore-you-dont-own-me-american-anthem.
3. "You Don't Own Me." Genius. Accessed August 7, 2019. https://genius.com/Lesley-gore-you-dont-own-me-lyrics.

"Four Women"
1. "Four Women." Genius. Accessed August 7, 2019. https://genius.com/Nina-simone-four-women-lyrics.
2. Himes, Geoffrey. "'Four Women' channels Nina Simone's protest music." The Washington Post. Last modified November 2, 2017. Accessed July 18, 2019. https://www.washingtonpost.com/goingoutguide/theater-dance/four-women-channels-nina-simones-protest-music/2017/11/01/904d9f6a-bb32-11e7-a908-a3470754bbb9_story.html?noredirect=on&utm_term=.c1c7438f227b.
3. Roth Pierpont, Claudia. "A Raised Voice." The New Yorker. Last modified August 3, 2014. Accessed July 18, 2019. https://www.newyorker.com/magazine/2014/08/11/raised-voice.

"Respect" and "I Am Woman"
1. Capatides, Christina. "How Aretha Franklin turned 'Respect' into one of the most powerful female anthems of all time." CBS News. Last modified August 16, 2018. Accessed July 18, 2019. https://www.cbsnews.com/news/untold-history-behind-aretha-franklin-respect/.
2. "I Am Woman." Genius. Accessed August 7, 2019. https://genius.com/Helen-reddy-i-am-woman-lyrics.
3. "Respect." Genius. Accessed August 7, 2019. https://genius.com/Aretha-franklin-respect-lyrics.
4. Salam, Maya. "What Is the Equal Rights Amendment, and Why Are We Talking About It Now?" The New York Times. Last modified February 22, 2019. Accessed July 18, 2019. https://www.nytimes.com/2019/02/22/us/equal-rights-amendment-what-is-it.html.
5. Ulaby, Neda. "You're Gonna Hear Them Roar: 'I Am Woman' Is An Anthem Beyond Its Era." NPR. Last modified October 24, 2018. Accessed July 18, 2019. https://www.npr.org/2018/10/24/651795560/i-am-woman-helen-reddy-american-anthem-hear-them-roar.
6. Alice Paul Institute. "ERA Frequently Asked Questions." ERA. Accessed August 7, 2019. https://www.equalrightsamendment.org/faq.

"The Pill"
1. "Griswold v. Connecticut." Oyez. Accessed May 23, 2019. https://www.oyez.org/cases/1964/496.
2. Megginson, Tom. "At 40, Loretta Lynn's 'The Pill' is still crucial social marketing." Osocio. Last modified March 13, 2012. Accessed July 18, 2019. https://osocio.org/message/at-40-loretta-lynns-the-pill-is-still-crucial-social-marketing/.
3. "Roe v. Wade." Oyez. Accessed April 18, 2019. https://www.oyez.org/cases/1971/70-18.
4. Talbot, Margaret. "Loretta Lynn, 'The Pill.'" The New Yorker. Last modified June 19, 2018. Accessed July 18, 2019. https://www.newyorker.com/recommends/listen/loretta-lynn-the-pill.
5. "The Pill." Genius. Accessed August 7, 2019. https://genius.com/Loretta-lynn-the-pill-lyrics.

"Standing on the Shoulders" and "Rebel Girl"

1. "19th Amendment 75th Anniversary Rally." Video file, 1:56:00. C-SPAN. August 26, 1995. Accessed July 18, 2019. https://www.c-span.org/video/?66864-1/19th-amendment-75th-anniversary-rally.
2. Johnson Rouse, Joyce. "Standing on the Shoulders." Earth Mama. Last modified 1995. Accessed December 15, 2019. https://earthmama.org/wp-content/uploads/2019/03/standing_on_the_shoulders_144.pdf and www.StandingOnTheShoulders.org.
3. Rampton, Martha. "Four Waves of Feminism." Pacific, Fall 2008. Accessed July 18, 2019. https://www.pacificu.edu/about/media/four-waves-feminism.
4. "Rebel Girl." Genius. Accessed August 7, 2019. https://genius.com/Bikini-kill-Rebel-girl-lyrics.
5. Smith, Rachel. "Revolution Girl Style, 20 Years Later." NPR. Last modified September 22, 2011. Accessed July 18, 2019. https://www.npr.org/sections/therecord/2011/09/20/140640502/revolution-girl-style-20-years-later.

"Hijabi"

1. Davis, Lelia A., "Woman's dress, a question of the day," Dept. of Hygiene and Heredity, Provincial W.C.T.U. 1894. Accessed July 26, 2019. http://eco.canadiana.ca/view/oocihm.91023.
2. "Hijabi." Genius. Accessed August 7, 2019. https://genius.com/Mona-haydar-hijabi-lyrics.
3. Jones, Sasha. "Do School Dress Codes Discriminate Against Girls?" *Education Week*. Last modified August 31, 2018. Accessed July 26, 2019. https://www.edweek.org/ew/articles/2018/09/05/do-school-dress-codes-discrimate-against-girls.html.
4. Radioff, Jessica, "Syrian American Activist Mona Haydar Has a Powerful Reason for Wearing a Hijab," Glamour, April 25, 2017. Accessed July 26, 2019. https://www.glamour.com/story/syrian-american-activist-mona-haydar-has-a-powerful-reason-for-wearing-a-hijab.
5. Taylor, Michael and Kanso, Heba, "New Zealand women face praise and protests for donning the hijab," Reuters. March 26, 2019. Accessed July 27, 2019. https://www.reuters.com/article/us-newzealand-shootout-headscarves/new-zealand-women-face-praise-and-protests-for-donning-the-hijab-idUSKCN1R71Q9.

"Woman"
1. Blanchard, Emma. "Kesha Drops a Donald Trump Inspired Song." *V magazine*. Last modified July 13, 2017. Accessed July 20, 2019. https://vmagazine.com/article/kesha-drops-donald-trump-inspired-song/.
2. Hogan, Marc. "The Ugly State of Kesha and Dr. Luke's Never-Ending Legal Battle." *Pitchfork*. Last modified August 31, 2018. Accessed July 20, 2019. https://pitchfork.com/thepitch/the-ugly-state-of-kesha-and-dr-lukes-never-ending-legal-battle/.
3. Johnston, Maura. "Kesha and Dr. Luke: Everything You Need to Know to Understand the Case." Rolling Stone. Last modified February 22, 2016. Accessed July 20, 2019. https://www.rollingstone.com/music/music-news/kesha-and-dr-luke-everything-you-need-to-know-to-understand-the-case-106731/.
4. "Woman." Genius. Accessed August 7, 2019. https://genius.com/Kesha-woman-lyrics.

Postlude
1. Klinghoffer, Judith Apter and Elkis, Lois. "'The Petticoat Electors': Women's Suffrage in New Jersey, 1776-1807." Journal of the Early Republic, Vol. 12, No. 2 (Summer 1992), p. 159-193.
2. Women in Elective Office 2019, Center for American Women and Politics, Rutgers Eagleton Institute of Politics. Accessed July 28, 2019. https://www.cawp.rutgers.edu/women-elective-office-2019.

About the League of Women Voters

THE LEAGUE OF WOMEN VOTERS was founded by Carrie Chapman Catt in 1920 during the convention of the National American Woman Suffrage Association. The convention was held just six months before the Nineteenth Amendment to the U.S. Constitution was ratified, giving women the right to vote after a seventy-two-year struggle.

From the beginning, the League has been an activist, grassroots organization whose leaders believed that citizens should play a critical role in advocacy. It was then, as it is now, a nonpartisan organization. League founders believed that maintaining a nonpartisan stance would protect the fledgling organization from becoming mired in the party politics of the day. However, League members were encouraged to be political themselves, by educating citizens about, and lobbying for, government and social reform legislation.

Carrie Chapman Catt. (National Nineteenth Amendment Society)

This holds true today. The League is proud to be nonpartisan, neither supporting nor opposing candidates or political parties at any level of government, but always working on vital issues of concern to members and the public. The League has a long, rich history that continues with each passing year.

Made in the USA
Columbia, SC
03 April 2020